Penworthy 10-11-88

612010

Once There Was a
Seed

For Nellie - J.A.

For Caiden, Lucy, and Ben - M.G.

First edition for the United States, its territories and
dependencies, and Canada published in 2010 by
Barron's Educational Series, Inc.

First published in 2009 by Wayland
Copyright © Wayland 2009

Wayland
338 Euston Road, London, NW1 3BH

All inquiries should be addressed to:
Barron's Educational Series, Inc.
250 Wireless Boulevard, Hauppauge, NY 11788
www.barronseduc.com

The right of Judith Anderson to be identified as the author
of the work has been asserted by her in accordance with
the Copyright, Designs, and Patents Act 1988.

Editor: Nicole Edwards • Designer: Paul Cherrill
Digital Color: Carl Gordon

Library of Congress Control Number: 2009933530

ISBN-13: 978-0-7641-4493-6
ISBN-10: 0-7641-4493-6

Date of Manufacture: December 2009
Manufactured by: WKT, Shenzhen, China

Printed in China
9 8 7 6 5 4 3 2 1

Nature's Miracles

Once There Was a
Seed

Written by
Judith Anderson

Illustrated by
Mike Gordon

BARRON'S

Grandpa loves
growing things.

He says he has a green thumb. He says I have a green thumb, too.

"Having a green thumb" means being good at growing things.

Today we're going to
plant some seeds.

First we push the seeds
into some soil.

Grandpa says that seeds
need three things to grow.

They need water,
warmth, and light.

When a seed has water and warmth, a little root starts to grow out of it.

Oh yes...

Is it growing yet?

10

The root grows downward.

Like this?

That's right!

Next, a little shoot grows
out of the seed. The shoot
grows upward.

When it reaches the light,
it starts to sprout leaves.

Grandpa says plants are just
like us. They need food to grow.
We get our food at meal times.
Plants make their own food
from water, light, and air.

Below the soil, the roots
are getting bigger and
spreading further.

Above the soil, the plant is growing taller.

Amazing!

When the plant is big enough,
some new buds appear.

These buds turn into flowers.

Flowers come in many colors
and shapes. Some smell sweet,
too. Grandpa says that his
flowers look and smell so good
that he might win a prize at the
flower show.

But I think it is so that
insects will notice them.

Mmm! My
favorite!

Flowers contain pollen.
When an insect visits
a flower, pollen sticks
to its body.

When the insect flies to another flower, the pollen goes, too.

It's not dust, it's pollen!

One flower swaps pollen with another flower. Then the flower dies, but it leaves new seeds behind.

Apple seeds are called **pips!**

Before seeds grow into new plants, they need to find their own patch of soil. Often they are carried by the wind.

Sometimes a bird
helps them.

Sometimes
a squirrel
helps them.

27

And sometimes
Grandpa helps them.

NOTES FOR PARENTS AND TEACHERS

Suggestions for reading the book with children

As you read this book with children, you may find it helpful to stop and discuss what is happening page by page. Children might like to talk about what the pictures show, and point out the changes taking place in the plants and trees. What other types of leaves, flowers, fruits, and seeds are they familiar with?

The idea of a life cycle is developed throughout the book, and reinforced on the final pages when it becomes clear that the plant that was once a seed has now produced seeds of its own. Ask the children if they know of any other life cycles. Can they see any patterns in nature? The other titles in the series may help them think about this.

Discussing the subject of seeds and plants may introduce children to a number of unfamiliar words, including root, shoot, bud, and pollen. Make a list of new words and discuss what they mean.

Nature's Miracles

There are four titles about life cycles in the **Nature's Miracles** series: *Once There Was a Seed; Once There Was a Caterpillar; Once There Was a Tadpole;* and *Once There Was a Raindrop.* Each book encourages children to explore the natural world for themselves through direct observation and specific activities and emphasizes developing a sense of responsibility toward plants, animals, and natural resources.

Once There Was a Seed will help young readers to think about conditions for growth and stages of growth.

Suggestions for follow-up activities

The little girl in this book plants a seed and watches it grow. Planting seeds and caring for young plants is a fun and rewarding activity, whether you have access to a garden or not. All you need are some seeds, a container, and a growing medium — it doesn't even have to be soil. A carrot top in a saucer of water or cress seeds sprinkled on a damp tissue all help to demonstrate the need for light, warmth, and water.

Choosing which seeds or plants to grow can be great fun, and it encourages children to think about variety and habitat. Do you have enough space for sunflowers? Bulbs such as daffodils might make an interesting alternative. Would vegetables or fruit be a good idea? Seed potatoes will grow in a pot if it is large enough, as will tomatoes.

Once the seeds or bulbs have been planted, explain that it may take some time before a shoot appears. Encourage children to think about warmth, light, and water. How much does the plant need? Can it have too much? Is there anything else that might harm the plant's chances to grow?

Further reading

Little Box of Gardening, by Louise Rooney, illustrated by Julie Clough. (Barron's Educational Series, Inc., 2001)
Why Should I Protect Nature? by Jen Green, illustrated by Mike Gordon. (Barron's Educational Series, Inc., 2005)

Useful websites

www.hortikids.com/
www.kidsgardening.com
http://eartheasy.com/grow_gardening_children.htm

Index